Published by
All's Well That's Maxwell
New Haven, CT

ISBN-13: 978-0-9915544-0-9
ISBN-10: 099155440X

First Times.

Thank you to everyone who was brave enough not only to submit their stories, but also to write them.

I.

Mazzy

I popped in a tampon for the first time in the Spring of 2009 under the didactic guidance of three girls who rushed me to the third floor bathroom of the Nightingale-Bamford School and imposed a five-minute lockdown within it: they decreed that no one should, nor could, enter. We were in Class XII, which is not a class, but an entire grade, and in my year, one filled with thirty-seven girls.

As of 1980, tampons have been classified as a Class II medical device. The process of relegating seemingly simple human processes and objects to the medical world is a common theme I noticed in my Biology of Women class, first semester of freshman year at Wesleyan University. French for *stamp, plug,* or *stopper,* the antiseptic cotton tampon was employed in the 1800s to quell bleeding from bullet shots (it isn't uncommon to hear of current soldiers who might use them for the same reason as well). The ancient Egyptians employed softened papyrus, the ancient Greeks draped wood with lint, and the ancient non-Egyptians and non-Greeks employed wool, vegetable fibers, sponges, paper, and grass as the contents of a tampon, or as makeshift tampons in and of themselves. In medieval Islam, they were used as contraceptive devices. And after this, a reusable cloth rag saw you through those five to seven days every month.

Sam Hall, who, in senior year of high school, insisted we address her as Samantha, told us stories that were not unremarkable. We shared a peer group. We were in seventh grade. And there is one of two memorable stories that I wish to recount, and it is not the one about her grandmother who, believed to have passed away, suddenly arose upon hearing "Who wants this cookie?" The story I'm interested in involves a girl sauntering in a bikini, an incredibly curious boy, and a string dangling from her bikini bottom. I cringed because it sounded like it could be painful. The other girls cringed because they knew it was. I was not part of the inclusive grandeur that was being an Experienced Girl. Telling someone I don't know how to swim tends to elicit bafflement and amusement. Telling someone I had never used a tampon elicits an equally shocked, yet completely different reaction.

By using a tampon, you are distancing yourself from the menstrual process, plugging and shoving and absorbing. Yet using a digital tampon--one sold without a plastic applicator that is unwrapped and pushed into the vagina--is environmentally sound and seems to somehow be more personal; it is just you, cotton, and the string. Whereas applicator tampons expand axially, or in length, digital kinds expand radially, or in diameter. The most common digital brand is o.b., which in German is "Ohne Binde" and translates to "without a pad." They are significantly more inexpensive than the Tampax ones with the plastic applicator, but Papa still brought home economy-sized Kotex pads from Costco and that was The Way. My mother—who my sister and I always called Mimi and as of recently, Mims—equates the insertion of a tampon to that of a penis, to the motions of one losing her virginity. And who uses them, Mims? The bad girls, white girls, advanced girls, *bideshees* (Americans). My sister and I did not question their absence in our household bathroom cabinets, but unlike other Forbidden Things that we actively sought out, the violent mass of cotton and rayon in the plastic applicator did not interest us, and we were, quite frankly, scared of them.

Bhanu Kapil Rider writes, "To cube life. Because we can't take it—in a whole form." I ripped open the camel-colored wrapper on a cigarette and said the filter remarkably resembled a cotton tampon. My friend Eduardo agreed. I thought, Look at me! I am cubing life; I am fragmenting it from its form! The other day I looked at a packet of incense and said it resembled the plastic wrapper of a tampon. My friend Franz agreed. But Jamie said boys don't go around talking about ejaculation to girls, so why should girls talk periods all casual like that?

A slow movement from the emergency room and the faster movement there, the porous nature of sleep, sleep paralysis, a stalker sending photographs to yours truly that were not perverted, hives and the chunky welts it left like gifts—these are the plagues of freshman year at Wesleyan, the year I handed my friend, who would stay on campus over the summer, a plastic bag full of items that I did not want my mother to see: issues of the school's art and sexuality magazine, lighters, certain photographs, a box of tampons.

In my parents' bedroom there is a drawer in which my mother stashes things that she does not want me to see. Two items I can think of: year-old cigarettes she confiscated from me and the phone number of Ajmeri Baba, the long-distance astrologer she secretly calls at night. Every now and then I look in the drawer to ensure that the cigarettes are there. I wonder why she clings to these, why the Museum of Menstruation was only open from 1994 to 1998 and why I had not heard about it from friends (had any visited?), why there is no Museum of Ejaculation, if I would sleep with a tampon in even though I've been erroneously told this should *not* be done and how I violate that rule when it comes to contact lenses anyway, but really, I wonder why this summer I found a box of currently-being-used o.b. tampons in Mims' drawer, under her address books and prayers.

Looking like bullets, being used to treat wounds from bullets. See the wounds; they may be shaped like bullets, too.

II.

Claire

Hi Claire,

Last night Genevieve, Mallory & I watched Sunday Night Football. In the middle of the game, Genevieve noticed an unusual (bad) smell. Mallory volunteered that the odor was likely the vaginal discharge in her underwear. She then showed it to Genevieve. She said she was wearing your underwear by the way. Mom had no interest in talking to Mallory about it & Genevieve was more overcome by the odor. Therefore, as a big sis you need to call Mallory tonite & explain what's going on & what to do to prepare for her time of the month.

Please call Mallory tonite. It's your duty!
XO

At first, I had no idea what my father was referring to. After a few seconds, I realized my younger sister had received her first period. I had never mentioned a period to anyone in my family. In fact, the first two years after I received my first period I wore panty liners because I did not know about the existence of pads and I could not figure out a tampon. I told nobody about my maturation—including my older sister, Genevieve, and my mother. I was too embarrassed.

However, my younger sister had been thrilled about the prospect of her period. She would bring it up all of the time while the rest of the family would cringe in embarrassment. At the dinner table she would tell us how excited she was to finally become a woman and how she hoped her boobs would grow to B's eventually. The rest of us would exchange awkward glances while her twin, Matt, would yell at her to shut up. Nobody really knew how to deal with her sexuality since the rest of us hid ours so well.

At the beginning of my sophomore year in college, I received a phone call from Mallory. I paced the steps outside of the library trying to extract myself from the phone conversation. Mallory had discharged something, but it was not blood, and she was severely disappointed. Apparently my mother had told her to call Genevieve, who then told her to call me. I could not sympathize with her. For the life of me I could not understand why she would want to share this news with the world.

Over Fall break I was in the car with Genevieve and Mallory on the way to the supermarket. "Guys! Check this out!" Genevieve and I both turn around to see Mallory with her shorts and underwear off,

4

exposing herself completely. "Look! Black hair is growing!" Cheeks growing bright red, Genevieve and I quickly turn to face front.

"Mallory! Cover up! That's disgusting," Genevieve tells her.

"But it's exciting!" Nothing could deter Mallory's excitement.

I received the e-mail from my father on November 11, 2012. I made a point not to call home for the next week. I did not want to hear how things were going. I cringed at the thought of explaining to Mallory how to deal with a period. I hoped my mom or Genevieve would grow the balls to help her out. I decided the best course of action would be to ignore my Dad's e-mail and hope for the best. My "duty?" I thought he was crazy. I figured that if I could eventually figure out pads and tampons, so could she.

A few days after coming home for Winter Break, I was in my room trolling the internet for summer internships. "Claire?" I hear a squeaky little voice say, and see Mallory peering around my door. "Is it normal to have a period for four days?" She whispers, fear in her voice.

I feel my face reddening. "Yes, Mallory. Seven days is actually normal."

"Well, I don't know where to wear the pads."

"What do you mean?"

"I covered my underwear with four pads but no more will fit. I don't know where on the underwear they're supposed to go. I can't tell where the red is coming from." She pulls down her pants, and to my surprise, she was wearing four pads, in a crisscross formation. "I switch them every two hours because the internet said so. Dad took me to the store and waited in the car while I went in and bought four packages of pads."

I groan, unsure of what to do. I've never dealt with somebody else's private parts. "Mallory, you wear one pad on the bottom of your underwear. And you change it when it needs to be changed, it's not according to a certain time. Any other questions, please direct to Genevieve. Please never tell anyone we talked about this."

Mallory solemnly nods, knowing not to mention our conversation to anyone. We now share a secret that our family will never learn. Family values teach us our bodies are private, both in discussion and physicality.

We always joke that Mallory is going to end up the nudist of the family, while she was merely doing what any regular pre-teenager would do when getting her period. I never mentioned my conversation with Mallory to anyone else in the family. I don't know if she knows what a tampon is. I think it's Genevieve's turn to tell her about that.

I still receive monthly text messages from Mallory saying, "I'm not pregnant!" She finds the joke hysterical. I have yet to respond to one of those texts. I wonder how my dad feels about her saying it at the dinner table. My mom mentioned on the phone how Mallory brought up buying new pads while my grandparents were over and my grandpa choked up his whiskey. Forever in WASP-land.

III.

Christian

Rank and file. All of us were just standing there, rank and file, us innocent 16-year-old high school boys, me and my friends, each of us individually calculating how to best build our own sexual résumé. None of us understood the concept of having a female friend, let alone the concept of "wingmanning." Nope, everybody for themselves. Go procure your own handjob, and report back for those of us that haven't had one yet. Rank and file, ready to defile.

I was moving along like any one of the guys could have hoped for, albeit slowly, with my girlfriend of a few months, Denise. And it was the best that I could have hoped for too: I could finally say to myself, "16's not too late to see my first set of nipples, right?" Come to think of it, Denise was a whole world of first times. She was my first text message fight, my first blowjob, the first girl I ever bought roses, and the first for a whole lot of other shit that I would hope for any American teenager to experience in high school. Denise and I didn't relate on an intensely personal level; she was more of an "I love to dance in the rain!" sort of girl, and I a more subtle kid. We were not best friends, but she was a sweetheart nonetheless.

It was Denise that had initiated the let's-undo-the-belt thing, and I can remember the first time she touched my cock. It was around two months before my 17th birthday. I had touched it many times, many, many times before, but the second she undid my zipper it was different. Neither of us had ever cum for another person before, and sex and jizz and titjobs and facials were, for me, reserved for Internet porn stars and my parents. Just Denise's touch had been as satisfying as any blowjob could have been. Like I said, we were moving slowly, but I knew that we'd make some serious progress on my birthday.

Fast forward to my birthday. Denise was on one of her pissy benders, and she was not one to wear a sweatshirt when she had emotions on her sleeve. But that helped me, her, and my friends Dan and Little Frank (he's Taiwanese, we call him Asian/Little Frank), to have an extremely awkward dinner at Buffalo Wild Wings in celebration of both my 17th birthday and my implied, imminent introduction to vagina. I will admit, there's a gap in my memory between dinner and the backseat of my parents' Hyundai Sonata, the scene of 95% of our sexual encounters. I had the spot all planned out – the rubble construction lot on the premises of an all-girls Catholic high school, Woodlands Academy. It was a sweaty, mosquitoey night. It was the sort of night that's almost too easy to describe because everyone but an Inuit knows what an incredibly humid night is like. To this day I wonder about the amount of dehydrated sweat still lurking within the threads of the cloth seats. With both rear doors open, we were lying horizontally across the back row, and I took the first step towards making sure that we ended up sans-pantaloons, unbuckling her belt. She helped take off her skintight navy blue jeans, unveiling a tasteful white thong in the process. Her legs were cooler than any other part of her body accessible to me.

It was time to grow up, I had decided, after all I was *17* goddamned years old! So I obtained consent to stuff my nose into her pussy, which was quickly granted, and I proceeded to eat my first box in a manner solely based upon a scene from the movie *American Pie*. I can specifically remember the taste as being almost sweet, but oddly tangy, much like a Swedish fish that had a drop of hand soap on it. Denise had the moans down. It was the kinkiest thing I had ever done in my life thus far besides jerking off six times in one day. Her hands were grasping the thick air outside the car when I stuck a finger in. It was the first time I had done that too. I felt a small string and a plastic like object, but I had never stuck a finger up a vagina before, so I surely was no expert on what vaginas should feel like. I kept with that for a few seconds more, and when it was her turn to show me her moves, they were much more tame.

Months later, I put two and two together, the same two and two that you've probably gathered from my description my old girlfriend's vagina. Yes, she had been on her period. But it was still fucking kinky. And no matter how prude we were, we still thought of each other as kinks, although I may have left out the period detail when reporting back to the rank and file friends.

IV.

Chris

"Have you ever been eaten out?" I whispered the question with hot breath into her ear, trying to sound cool. "No," she giggled, uncertain where I was going with this. "Well, I will," I said with a cool conviction. I was a veritable gun-slinging Eastwood who had just shot and killed his last victim in a classic Spaghetti Western, the final shot, my mouth, your vagina.

I nosed on down her body, sucking her nipples, kissing her abdomen, and finally her legs. I had seen this all before in pornos, and my older friends in school told me about the process with fiery delight in its effect to make them "all squeamish and ticklish." And then it was there, all gnarled in pink skin, like tissue paper that had been left in my pocket for too long, finally taken out, steeped in whatever scent that was, maybe like an orange slice left out in the sun for a day, with bleach poured over it. And then with a vagina square between my eyes, my surrounding all of a sudden seemed a little bit more fucked up – a public bathroom in a trailer park. I shimmied back up her body to meet my lips to hers. "Why don't you just give me a blowjob?" I asked. No, this is not a story about my first muff dive, but rather a fateful blowjob.

I hadn't at that point acquired my father's sentiment that "the vagina is like a fine burgundy, it only gets better with age." In a similar vain, I didn't like coffee growing up, but now I like it. I also like cunnilingus now—I guess that just came with age. When I told him about my blowjob, my dad told me everything. It was like he had been waiting to tell me about all of his tips and tricks. You might ask, why on earth would you ever tell your dad about your first blowjob. Well, it wasn't out of choice you see, it's because I thought—or at least I was told—that I had gonorrhea. So this isn't even a story about a blowjob, necessarily, but rather about the first time I thought I had an STD—that abortion of a disease, proof that god hates us and wants us to be miserable. Because, in the end, it was just a blowjob, a first one at that. And they're all really the same. Penis in her mouth, her mouth around my penis, some slight pain, some considerable pain, and there, "whala" the band aid is ripped off and you've cum in her mouth, a then there, "whala," "gulp" she's swallowed it. And then "Ohh my god what the fuck am I doing, where I am I, my cum went where? Eww she wants to kiss me now?" "Umm, I should go," panic, shower and wash penis and body in another public shower room, hope that she doesn't see me when she comes out.

"Yup," the text read. "You gave me gonorrhea. I have bumps in the back of my throat." It was my first blowjob ever and her second. This was an entirely possible situation. "Yup," my dad said to me when I told him. "I had it once. Broke up with the girl after. But don't worry you just get some pills and it goes away."

The doctor was stoical and I was not. I sprawled out on the neoprene bed, crinkling the wax paper, ranting off instances of promiscuity and what instances I had gathered from the girl. "Well, she had only given one blowjob before, but she said her boyfriend cheated on her and got a blowjob from this other girl, so maybe…" The stoical man had gone to medical school for this. But apparently not "I'm not going to go around turning up stones to find out what you acquired in, what was it? A public shower?"

I talked to her every two days or so. "So, how's your gonorrhea?" I would ask, imagining the sores, wanting to ask for a picture of her throat.

"They're gone now," she told me one day. "Yea, I took some antibiotics and they went away…. Ohh, and it wasn't gonorrhea, I just had strep throat, at least according to the school nurse."

"When did you find this out?"

"Like three days after I told you I had gonorrhea."

"And why didn't you tell me? I went to the doctor, I told my dad, I've been freaking out since I came in your mouth!"

"You didn't go down on me in the shower, I don't know I just thought it was appropriate."

I was mad, and I vented to my dad who again reminded me "well don't feel so bad, I actually had it." So in the end, it all wasn't so bad. I learned some cool things about my dad and we were able to bond.

V.

Bella

As a rule, I don't interact with straight males. Throughout middle and high school, I'd say that I was friendly to the guys in my class and was usually well-respected by them, but I can't say I was ever good friends with them, except for Andy, who came out of the closet the year after we graduated high school. On the other hand, I was always great friends with basically all the girls. Not that I was a huge lesbian or transgender or anything like at all; in fact, since elementary school, I tended to get obsessive crushes on boys. Whether it was Josh Gurshiwitz my beautiful b'nai mitzvah partner whom I could only talk to at b'nai mitzvah rehearsal, or David Sandler, the half-Asian Jew who bought me a pair of blue and yellow Nike sneakers in 11th grade that I still wear, I have always had a long list of boys that I say I'm "in love with" but aren't even really able to talk to let alone look in the eye.

In 10th grade, I really hit rock bottom. His name was Aaron Moskowitz, and he was the most amazing boy I had ever met. He had the most beautifully striking blue eyes and in my eyes, was utterly perfect. He was in 11th grade at the time, an older man. I met him in Houston BBYO, B'nai B'rith Youth Organization, the Jewish youth group I was involved in throughout high school. Everyone who wanted a place in the Houston Jewish Community had to join BBYO. Aaron was president of his boy's chapter, and I was in charge of programming for my girl's chapter, so we had to work together to plan a program, specifically a mall "Jewish Love Day Scavenger Hunt." As a Jewish youth group, we had to call Valentine's Day "Jewish Love Day."

Anyway, since our first meeting, I was captivated by him. I had just gotten a Facebook, and every free moment I had I spent stalking him and looking at his photos. Every day after I got home, I would get online to see if earthtoaaron2002 was online. We didn't talk outside of our meetings or our two-minute instant messaging chats. However, I was convinced we had something special, so I asked him via AIM to come watch me in the upcoming performance of Chekhov's *The Good Doctor*. He agreed to come. I wouldn't learn about the true implications of heteronormitivity or gender norms for a few years so I thought that after the performance would be a good time to tell him that I liked him, like, liked him liked him. I sure had guts. I was so sure he'd love my performance as a shrieking crazy cat lady and afterwards find me utterly irresistible that he would have to say he liked me back! Backstage during the performance, I kept replaying the looming confrontation in my head and consulting my peers for advice. They told me to just go for it, and after the play, I nervously walked outside to find Aaron.

To be honest, I'm not completely sure of the exact conversation we had, but this is what I do remember. I awkwardly found Aaron, and we started walking towards the doors of my high school. After making small talk for a little bit, I think I said to him, "So I think I like you, like more than a friend." And he said something like, "I like you too, but not like that." I think I was so embarrassed that I missed the rest of the conversation because all I remember happening after that was getting a phone call from him at our IHOP cast party when he told me again that "I think we should just be friends," to which I replied "Ok bye I'll talk to you later!" And then I didn't really talk to him for over two years; every time I would run into him at a youth group function, I would look the other way and say nothing. When I saw him with his whole family when I was at brunch at Houston's New York Bagel Shop one Sunday morning, I immediately ran into the bathroom and called my friend for advice before facing him and saying solely "Hi, how are you? Bye." I hadn't talked to him since, until he came into Red Mango last summer while I was working to purchase frozen yogurt, three small Madagascar Vanillas with mangos on top. This could be my future: serving frozen yogurt to Aaron Moskowitz and the other men who have rejected me.

That was the first time that I ever told a boy that I liked him.

VI.

Julius

I was 16. My NFTY group all met in the airport for our group trip to Israel. My boy, Willy and I were pumped to meet girls and get our dicks wet. Before we did anything, we started spitting game at two girls in the airport, Jenna and Carly, who were going to be on our flight. I figured I obviously couldn't do anything with them, it's just good practice. So we get on the plane and see these girls are sitting a few rows behind us. So we made some trades and ended up sitting next to them. I was talking to Jenna, Willy was talking to Carly. I think Willy was stoned or something because he didn't seem too attentive. Meanwhile I was charming the fuck out of my girl. Next thing you know we are making out in the middle of this plane to Israel while Willy and Carly are watching awkwardly... So Jenna says to me "it's a 12 hour flight, I'm gonna go back to my seat and take a nap then come back." So I just chilled and drifted off. 45 minutes later Jenna comes and wakes me up. "My friend wants you"... "Huh?"... "My friend wants you... so she's gonna come instead of me." Carly came back to my seat, and that is the story of the first, and only time I got a blowjob on an airplane.

VII.

Rebecca

As the person with whom you asked to speak tonight, I hereby convene this hearing. The purpose of this hearing is straightforward. I want to get information and I want to get it face-to-face so as to avoid any ambiguity and/or future over-analysis. If I am to achieve that objective, a simple, not-asking-a-lot-objective, then you must show up. Seriously, you're half an hour late. Failure to appear at this hearing will result in loud obscenities, tears, and excessive consumption of alcohol. While I wait, let's review your prior offenses.

I.   **DECEMBER 15, 2012: Failure to say goodbye.**

> We had previously agreed you would spend my last night on campus before   winter break with me; once on December 8, and again on the phone, December 14.
>
> Exhibit A: A text message I sent to you, December 14, 12:20 a.m.
>
> "FUCK I'VE BEEN IN THE LIBRARY FOR 12 HOURS AND NOW I'M LOCKED OUT OF MY ROOM BECAUSE ALICE BORROWED MY KEY BUT SHE'S NOT ANSWERING HER PHONE AND THE KEY MASTER IS MISSING AND MY NEIGHBORS AREN'T HOME AND I'M JUST HOVELING IN MY DOORWAY LIKE A VAGRANT. I'M STARTING TO MEOW ALOUD."
>
> Let the record show that at 12:25 a.m., you called me. You asked if I was OK. We discussed meowing and confirmed our meeting on the fifteenth.

II.   **DECEMBER 16, 2012: Failure to apologize and/or explain Offense I**

III.   **DECEMBER 17, 2012: Failure to give a satisfying explanation upon inquiry.**

> Exhibit B: A text message you sent me, December 17, 3:38 p.m.
>
> "Yeah, real sorry about that. I was just kind of sad and went to bed early. Do you ever feel stale?"

IV.   **DECEMBER 21, 2012: Failure to continue our text conversation.**

V. **DECEMBER 22, 2012-January 20, 2013: Failure to communicate at all.**

Resulting in,

VI. **DECEMBER 25, 2012: Failure to wish me a merry Christmas.**

VII. **JANUARY 11, 2013: Public indecency.**

Exhibit C: Photographs accessed via Facebook indicating you were out with a Megan O. and a Meaghan G. that night. In Photograph 3, you are shown holding your shirt up with one hand, and a lit cigarette with the other. Let the record show that Megan O. captioned Photograph 3, "Who knew J. was hiding a six pack?"

VIII. **JANUARY 20, 2013: Failure to respond when I told you I was back on campus.**

IX. **JANUARY 26, 2013: Verbal harassment.**

At 4:39 a.m. you left me a voicemail exactly one minute and fourteen seconds long. Exhibit D: Transcript of said voicemail.

"Hey H., I'm kinda at the casino right now. It's really badass, you should probably wake your stupid ass up right now and get to the FUCKING casino. I don't know what you're doing right now, hanging out in Middletown, CT which is all STUPID and SHIT. And we're fucking chilling at the casino right now and it's really sweet. So you should probably wake up out of your bed with the quilt that your granmammy made you, or whatever, and just get down here and be a badass. PiNOT Noir, whatever that means, that's what I heard and that's what I'm going to say to you. So call me back IMMEDIATELY. It's like five in the morning and this is like a chill time so JUST DO IT. YEAHHHH. WOOOOOO."

Let the record show that slurring was evident and that I know that you know I do not have access to a car and cannot even drive.

X. **JANUARY 26, 2013: Failure to apologize for Offense**

Imagine my surprise when, after eight counts of failure, one count of public indecency, and one count of verbal harassment, you asked if we could talk tonight. However, after an hour it appears tonight will culminate in your eleventh offense.

XI.   **JANUARY 30, 2013: Failure to appear for your hearing.**

As previously stated, if you fail to appear at this hearing I will be sentenced to scream the word "fuck" at least seven times, cry, and drink to excess. I will be forced to begin my sentence at this time.

VIII.

Sasha

"Who do you have a crush on?" My friend asked. You couldn't not-have a crush at camp. It was where kids swam out to the island to kiss and dared each other to confess secrets around the fire. Where all flirtations led up to the final dance, where first periods were had and breasts budded, where two day old couples brushed pinkies at morning meeting, and boys wrote lyrics on guitar.

I had made up my mind that my crush was Ed. He was nice and funny, but most importantly he was tall: a rarity among twelve-year-olds. As soon as I let it slip to my friend, she went to work. The next day she told me that she had told him what I told her, "And he wants to ask you out!"

I took the word of this unsolicited matchmaking service with a grain of salt. I couldn't believe that Ed would want me. My curly hair has recently been chopped above my ears and the humidity made it stick out like buttresses on each side of my face. I was always running out in the rain or putting my head under a sink, since my hair looked so much better when wet. The New Hampshire mosquitoes had also taken a particular liking to my face and peppered it with bites that I scratched into bloody scabs. I was also a good head taller than the other girls and twice as thick, with strong thighs and wide hips, all piled atop a pair of long feet. I had never been a skinny kid, a cute kid, a pretty kid, and I was happy to let a romance with Ed exist in my fantasies. I didn't think he would come up to me in the cafeteria, lead me outside to the pine trees, and ask if I would like to go out with him, but I said yes, and we walked back inside holding hands.

Ed was quite the Casanova at camp. I was his sixth girlfriend (he counted for me once). Some of his relationships lasted a month, some for a day, but he made me feel inadequate since he was my first, like there was shame in being a single twelve-year-old. With all his "experience," Ed knew exactly how to play the game. He soldered together a heart out of different reds in the stained glass studio and gave it to me. He told me I was beautiful and took me out on sailboats. I told him I was jealous of the previous six women he had dated and he assured me that they could not hold a candle to me in any respect. He assured me that I was by far the prettiest, smartest, most interesting, coolest, least overweight, clearest-skinned, best-dressed, least-irresponsible girl in the world.

Ed's words were kind and I needed them, but his actions did not speak as loudly. For the life of me, I could not get him to give me a kiss. Aspirant vixen that I was, hopped up on new confidence, I tried to lead him into private places. I desperately wanted to do what I had been practicing for so many months by kissing the soft of my wrist at night.

I would tell Ed that I had lost my ring beneath the deck and, wink wink, I was going to go look for it. He preferred to continue playing ping-pong until I had found it, he said.

I would squeeze his hand and then saunter off behind the boathouse, swinging my hips around, then stop and flip my poofy hair to shoot him a come-hither glance. He had already walked away towards the lake.

I led him outside during the final dance, telling him I needed to get water from an outdoor fountain. We walked side by side in silence, until I jutted my neck out and kissed him on the cheek. "Awwwww," he said. "Thank you." Then he walked on to the water fountain and back into the dance, leaving me blushing by the pachysandra.

Still, he was incredibly doting. "Ed really loves you," other girls would giggle. "Doesn't all that attention drive you crazy?" I was frustrated and guilty. Did Ed not like me as much as he said? Or was I being superficial? Was I rushing things? Did I just want him for his body? Did we need to get to know each other better before touching lips?

We decided to stay together after camp ended and see how we would work out "long distance." We actually lived only thirty minutes away from each other, but neither of us could drive, so he may well have been on the other side of the country. Ed called every night to tell me about his day and how much he loved me. After a while I actually asked him to stop calling so much, because I couldn't think of things to talk about.

Slightly wounded, Ed resigned to calling every other day. He told me how his tests went, how his friend Susan was mad at him, how his little sister was growing up, and about books he had read and movies he had seen. He would talk through until the next date, when my dad would drive me to his house, or his mom would drive him to my house, or both of our parents would drive us to see *School of Rock* at the megaplex. There were no kisses in the dark of the theater and I was on fire.

He sent me a basket of lotions and bath salts on Valentines Day, gave me a teddy bear he had sewn at the mall for my birthday, and brought me back a painted wooden cat from a family vacation to New Mexico.

We went on for eight months, making Ed my longest relationship until senior year of college.

We did actually kiss once in winter, my first kiss. We went around behind his house, through backyard swing sets and porches until we reached the Hudson River. We sat on a bench, watching our breath. We both inched towards each other for warmth. We pressed our cheeks together, our teeth chattering. We touched our numb noses. We fumbled for each other's fingers through our gloves. Our raw, chapped lips slowly met. His warmth was a jolt down my throat and I was giddy. He pulled away and smiled. We huddled close and trekked back to his kitchen for tea.

Ed seemed so devoted, so head over heels, that I never expected him to be the one to break it off. He said the distance was too much. I was devastated because I thought that I ought to be, so I ate ice cream and watched movies and cried and listened to Return of Saturn over and over again. I told myself I could relate to Gwen Stefani, which made me feel very adult indeed.

The lotion gift basket should have been a giveaway, but Ed turned out not to be interested in women. I heard that he played Angel in his high school production of *Rent*. We still lived half an hour apart from each other at that point, but we were probably worlds away. I still faced the challenges of being too tall and too wide, but who knows what kind of self-acceptance Ed had to learn. I don't know. Maybe it was easy for him to come out, since he was so charming. Maybe it was hard, since he rested on his reputation as a ladies man.

It's fine by me that I was his crutch, his cover story of "long-distance girlfriend." In retrospect, I don't doubt that he really did love me, even if it was platonically. He at least liked me a lot. What he gave me was, in some respects, much more sophisticated and deep than other relationships I have since been in, and he made my first kiss excite me for all those to follow.

IX.

R.E. King

I was half a world away and woke up sweating. I was lying down in my friend's apartment, sleeping on a pallet on her floor. The room was empty, a grey, dusky light filtering in through the window. I didn't know what time it was.

My hangover was gone, but my chest ached. The pain had jarred me from my nap. The country could do that to me sometimes, heat up my memories to a boil so I had to sweat them out in my sleep. Germany felt like a personal guilt sauna. There was just too much time: too much time to count your failures; too much time to critique and analyze the past; too much time to think about home. You prayed for the time to fall away, unnoticed. Every hour passed without much thought was a victory.

I hadn't heard from him in a year: Hank, my best friend from high school. I knew he was probably in his dorm room on the east coast or back home in Texas, but he could've been anywhere really. I didn't know; we hadn't talked. And that thought sickened me. Finally, after a year of unreturned calls and ignored texts I realized Hank had wrecked my heart. He'd wrecked it as bad as any hustler in lipstick and cheap heels.

I went out to the balcony and found I was alone. I took a swig from a Paulaner I hadn't finished the night before. The beer was flat, almost stale, and I tasted a little ash going down. I grimaced and put the bottle back on the table next to an ashtray overflowing with cigarettes. Across the street, the bus that ferried students over the Danube into the city choked to a stop, but no one got on. An ambulance siren wailed near the Uni and I looked to the west. The spring sunsets were a violent, beautiful thing in Passau. The sun looked like a massive blood orange caught in the trees.

Hank had wrecked my heart. That's the thought my mind kept circling back to. Hank had wrecked my heart. My best friend had been my first love and I had lost him. I hadn't been *in* love with Hank. I didn't have any sexual feelings for him or any other men. I wasn't a closet case from Texas finally realizing his sexual orientation during his semester abroad. But at that time, I hadn't ever loved a girl long enough to yearn for her after she was gone. Plus I had always assumed when you fell out of love with someone there would be this moment where you felt your heart cleave in two. There had to be an event where you could pinpoint the great shift between you and this other person, something that felt like the Milky Way rotating backwards.

I got up and took a bottle of beer from a case against the balcony railing. There were only six Paulaners left. I'd have to go to the Getränkemarkt before closing. Or was it after eight? It didn't matter; there was too much time anyway. In German when you asked for the time, you said "How late is it?", which I felt was closer to the truth. Everyday I woke up older. I was older after my nap than before it. Tonight I'd pass out on my bed, the floor spinning beneath me as if I were trying to stand on the earth's axis turning and I'd wake up the next morning...

I cracked open the beer on a table edge and took a long swig. At least Hank hadn't wrecked my heart all at once. He hadn't frozen it, then taken a hammer to it like he had with his high school sweetheart, Tess. They'd split after deciding to go to different schools in different states, but still had sex in Hank's Toyota anytime they were home. She still talked about Hank when he wasn't around. She still had the homecoming mum he had given her on her bedroom wall. I used to pity Tess. I had pitied the way she veiled the hurt of Hank's absence by imagining her future husband. I had pitied the way she couldn't understand how Hank wasn't built like that. I had pitied the way she couldn't get Hank was done with her. I took a sip from my beer. I thought about Hank and I moving into an apartment in Austin after graduation. I thought about working late with him and ordering pizza, while we chased our careers and the women we thought might make us better men. I thought about watching the Cowboys game with him while our wives gossiped about us on the porch and all the kids played in the yard. I thought about both of us being grey and slow and telling stories we couldn't remember over coffee at a Waffle House.

Suddenly, I heard the door of the apartment open behind me and I shredded all those dreams, erased every trace of them on my brain. I forgot them all on that balcony in Passau. I finished my beer and let the alcohol work its way into my blood until my heart felt dark and heavy like a grenade.

X.

Michael

The cheesy fries didn't stand a chance. Their numbers decimated in a matter of seconds, the few that remained sat lonely, strewn across the sticky table. Tom Petty twanged through speakers behind the bar. She said he was her favorite, so we stacked the jukebox with almost all of *Full Moon Fever*. This was a start.

The bros were with me, and we rarely missed when together. The don't hold back at all type crew. Loud and obnoxious may be no way to go through life, but it worked in our favor for those 4 hours.

We set up a shuffleboard game, so she pretty much had to talk to me. Power move. She rebuffed my "so what's your major" conversation in favor of the Jazzfest lineup. As a local girl, she thought northerners were funny, and excoriated me for my use of "wicked". That caught my attention because I thought everyone loved "wicked" as much as Dunkin Donuts. She didn't know what that was either. Somehow they pulled out a win on the shuffleboard table, but signed up to play again. This was progress.

The night free-fell to music, laughing, and dancing. As a sweaty dude, the New Orleans humidity in the spring was crushing me. I was drenched. I went home to clean up, and suggested I swing by her place. At the bar she claimed Robert Plant owned her couch. I didn't believe her, but wanted to see it.

As it turned out, the couch wasn't that comfortable, so we climbed upstairs. However after much gyration and struggle, my best efforts proved futile. Awesome. I went to the bathroom before submitting to the stupor. Didn't even try to hit the light. Was going to throw this down from memory.

In 5th grade, a health teacher described birth control to our class with vivid imagery, "picture putting a bag on a hose". One would be hard-pressed to find a more apt comparison to my crowning achievement of the academic quarter. I don't remember where it ended up.
As I spread-eagled into her bed, the ceiling fan announced itself. It screeched continuously, and would not stop. My hostess generously turned it off.

As the sun greeted the dilapidated campus housing, I awoke face-down. The sheets below me were wet. Wet sheets are rarely a good thing. I decided to see myself out on this one. I scampered out of the house, and began my journey home. That was the first date with my girlfriend of 2 years.

XI.

Alice

We celebrated at the 24-hour diner with onion rings, french toast and roast beef sandwiches; the late night dinner of champions.

I am always game to try new things, we both are pretty kinky. No whips or chains or anything, though we probably would be open to talking about it...

We spoke about anal sex once or twice, neither of us had strong feelings one way or the other.

We laughed off the idea...he is, simply put, very well endowed. It's like trying to put a square block in a circular hole-- it just wouldn't fit. He was scared of hurting me and I was plain scared. But I knew if I was going to try it, it would be with him.

I've heard everything, horror stories, stories of pleasure and stories of pain. Gay friends, straight friends, everyone has a story and everyone wants to share their words of wisdom. "Build up to it, start with a finger, then add one or two-- it's like stretching before running a race"; "Don't eat anything that makes you gassy for a few days and be sure you poop before you do it." I listened with an eager ear, but I wrote off their advice.

I was the little spoon, his hands began to explore my body. He knows every inch and every curve, but this was new. There was a little pressure; one finger, then two. Then we pulled out the lube.

I don't remember if one of us initiated it or it just happened, whatever it was we knew we were about to cross seriously uncharted territory. it wasn't awkward, it felt like the logical next step. Nothing about it was romantic or sexy, yet I have never felt more comfortable and secure around anyone.

Nearly an entire bottle of Astro glide later we collapsed down next to each other. Without missing a beat we hi-fived one another and began hysterically laughing in complete disbelieve and satisfaction.

We could now cross it off our bucket lists, we did it.

XII.

M.S.

The winter of 2010 was a typically cold winter, and I had just returned from school. At 15:00 the sun was already setting; the joy of living near the arctic circle. It was cold in the house because the architect of the building had designed our heaters to be inside the closets. I am not sure his meta-commentary on the comforts of a capitalist society were appropriate for a large family home. So, you could get warm clothing but to stay warm you'd have to change every 20 minutes (or camp out inside the closet, which was my modus operandi). My feet were dripping wet with melted ice water so I nestled into my parent's closet, mushed the shoe boxes and enjoyed the warmth for about a minute until my mother entered the room. She was on the phone with her sister.

"He had that whore in his car when he went to pick up Henry from his soccer match. It is not enough that he is fucking her and everyone knows about it, but now he is trying to replace me with her," she said to my aunt. I understood what she was saying. But I convinced myself it couldn't possibly be true. I had trouble comprehending that my parents existed in roles beyond those of just being my mother and father.

As a child, I wasn't prone to any dramatic behavior so, I stayed in the closet, silent, afraid to move because my mother had started crying and I didn't want her to feel ashamed, and I didn't know what to do with her tears. She would probably spank me for "spying" and send me along my way.

I was overcome with anger at her for exposing me to this betrayal and lovelessness. Both of my legs were going numb so I shifted ever so slightly, causing the shoe boxes to topple.

No hiding now.
I didn't sprint out or utter a word.
I stopped breathing for a moment.
Like prey. Hiding.
Staying still, I hoped she would ignore me so that I could then ignore the knowledge.

"I have to go," she said to my aunt.

Oh no.
My knowledge was about to be acknowledged.
She crawled over to the closet on all fours, and hugged me really tightly.

"I am so sorry. We're just adults, chatting. It is nothing."

I tried to backtrack to innocence but the tears had started flowing. I was crying out of confusion and this adult world I had all of a sudden been thrust into; I did not understand enough at that moment to be hurt. In hindsight, it doesn't matter anyway because I would have found out eventually – thus the consequences of my father's actions would not have changed depending on how I became aware of his philandering.

In those moments I felt no love for my father and that loss was so immense that it robbed me of any objectivity towards men for many years. I felt such a deep hatred for that specimen. Instead of loving attempts to get a rise out of me by my brothers, I saw mockery and condescension. No, I did not want my father to come to my dance recital; didn't he have *other* places to be? If my father had abandoned my mother, the person who bore his children, the woman who gave us life, why would he not abandon us, her products?

And he lied so well too!
I had never even suspected it!
Our culture had encouraged this.

To be a "man", you had to bring home the money and fuck a lot of women who weren't your wife. *Silence her with the power that centuries of patriarchal tradition had given you.* The fragile woman who was trying to assure me that my father was the heroic and virtuous man and pure beacon of love I thought him to be was the same person whom he had robbed of patience, and joy. One would think that at 10, a child should not have the full capacity to conceptualize and derive the full extent of this sort of betrayal. However, fights were an everyday occurrence at my house and the seeds of this betrayal had existed in every conversation had in my household; I simply hadn't noticed them hiding between the lines. They were served with morning tea and afternoon snacks and kisses goodnight.

My salient dreams had been encompassed in the seams of him teaching us how to swim and buying us ice cream and taking us on road trips but the apogees of his dalliances became the denouement of my iridescent consciousness. Meaning, the perverse maturity he had called adulthood consisted of thieving the women in his life of happiness; it meant lying and deceiving and shaming.

The loss of trust I felt that day in the most important man in my life, never went away. I had never before experienced such a loss of respect, such a deep confusion. My parents worked through it over the next decade. I do not know why my mom stayed, but I have many guesses. Most of them involve the words "community" and "coercion."

My first relationship and first love was marred by jealousy and possessiveness. After all, if a married man, a loving father, would carry on a multi-year affair then there was nothing stopping the man I was involved with from betraying my trust. My grand gestures to keep *this individual* in my life exceeded any promises I had made to myself. We had just hit the three year mark of our relationship and two of those years had been spent crawling around the country trying to see each other, attempts to ameliorate the difficulty of long distance, only to find out that goodbyes were always followed by tears and partings never got easier. Promises to never allow a man to dictate my decision-making were undermined by my offers to reject ambitious post-graduation job offers and move to brumal Chicago to be with him.

After three years our relationship was quickly devolving into constant fights and perpetual hurt feelings and I was desperate for it to survive because I needed that love and care and proof of reliability.

My grand gesture of moving to Chicago after college to save our relationship was rejected.

He said we would work it out.
He didn't want me tossing my future away.
I sprinted into the arms of some semi-anonymous man while traveling in the UK.
The bed was warm but uncomfortable.
He was sarcastic and demeaning.
I was sober.
He wanted to talk about investment banking in his thick German accent while making love *a collision of our bodies in contorted positions.*

I cheated on the dearest person in my life, closer than family or best friend.

Leaving the almost stranger's apartment in the cold misty London morning I wept, sitting on a bench in Hyde Park next to a sleeping homeless man, for doing to my love what my father had done to me; stolen innocence and faith in the ability of others to love truthfully and in our ability to love purely.

XIII.

Abigail

The first time life cut me a raw deal, I was 22. I suppose, in retrospect, that the deck had been stacked since I was 14, that being the year that I both developed C-cup breasts and found out my mom was diagnosed with breast cancer, two unrelated incidents that now seem to carry an almost symbolic weight and mysticism and might possibly serve as foreshadowing for the incidents to come eight years later. At the time, however, I was mostly into the idea of wearing shirts that showed my cleavage, a practice that had the dual benefit of making me feel like an adult woman and also grabbing the attention of the junior boys who hung out in the hallway between 3rd and 4th period classes. This attention was new to me, as previously the only stares I got were usually directed towards the Frida Kahlo that I sported fetchingly on my forehead. That year, my mom got sick, got surgery, got chemo, and began to get better. At the same time, I got my first boyfriend, (a junior, which made me a bit of a hero among the other freshman girls), got fingered for the first time, and went to junior prom. These incidents were also unrelated, and they carry none of the aforementioned symbolic weight and mysticism.

The deck being stacked, the stage being set for the raw deal, I continued throughout high school while my mom went into remission as I lived obliviously in my own world of friends, classwork, note-passing, and a series of ever-more-serious boyfriends who both entertained and infuriated me. The second one that came around was the first penis I put in my mouth, the one to follow swapped V-cards with me in a vodka-induced haze one summer afternoon on the floor of his brother's bedroom. It was after this series of boyfriends, and the backdrop of my teenage years set with hospital visits and platelet counts, that I found myself in the arms of a new boyfriend during my junior year of college. A month after we started dating, I got the call from home. My mom's cancer had morphed into something far more aggressive, more widespread, and more deadly. Talk had shifted from that of crushing the odds and successful remission to the more measured speech of chronic illness, of time left, of limited years.

Maybe it was the hope of relief from the heaviness that grew in my chest, but something propelled me full-steam into the center of this new relationship, despite obvious flaws from the outset, and with a passion hitherto inexperienced. I fell hard, into the twin sagas of lust and love.

That time doesn't matter now, it's a hazy series of generally happy images and sensations. There were lazy days in parks and on pillows, we ate grilled things, we swam in bodies of water, we swapped families and friends, engaging in all the other heartwarming activities that make up the world of two people in love. We talked about our futures, and he said things like, "you're the only thing I really care about," and "I want to spend as much time with you as possible," things that we meant fervently at the time. Then again, this was coming from someone incapable of getting his homework in on time, so with the 20/20 vision that comes with hindsight, it's clear that this theoretical future may have been compromised. We also had a lot of sex, probably excessive sex now that I think about it – probably an excessive enough amount of sex to cloud the vision of anyone, let alone two people in their early twenties.

What matters now is the raw deal- the fact that at 23 I found myself carrying the twin losses of my mother who had passed away, and now that of my cheating soon-to-be ex-boyfriend, who was in the process of telling me about the number of people he slept with while he was abroad as we sat in the car on a drive back from a particular northern city. We'd just made a pit stop at my family home to pick up all of his college stuff—boxes of clothes and dorm supplies and skateboards and detritus that he'd left at my place while he was away. The truth conveniently unveiled itself on our drive back to his college campus, from which I'd graduated a year earlier. Over the course of a 45-minute car ride, my reality crumbled at the seams and folded in on itself like a gaping, throbbing black hole, coming to settle at the center of my stomach. This sensation, I assure you, is quite unpleasant. The raw deal having been dealt, and the available course of immediate actions limited to sleeping either in my car or his college bedroom, I ended up lying next to him for one last night, wide awake, heart pounding with a fury and a power I'd never before experienced.

At the first sign of light in the sky, I threw open the shades and prodded him awake. We unloaded his boxes from my car and I left campus, headed out in the pale February sunrise and down I-95 towards New York City. I was headed to pick up two friends for our drive back to Washington, and I knew that if I could make it to them in one piece, everything would be okay. Or rather, that everything would collapse for a while, but that they would catch the scattered pieces of self that I dropped and hold onto them until I was ready to carry them once more.

I remember that drive so clearly; into the rising sun I spoke to myself, to the sky, the road, to whoever would listen: "I can do this, I am strong, this will not crush me, I will live on."

I remembered sitting next to my mom one night as she laid, bedbound, and telling her that my only fear was that she would slip from my life as she left her own behind. Her words to me were simple.

"I will always be with you in some way. Don't ever be scared of that. I have been there for you, I am here for you now, and I always will be."

On that drive I asked her, directing my words at some uncertain point in the distance between the clouds and the Manhattan skyline, "Mom, stay with me in this ride; I could use some of your strength."

Elizabeth

I remember so vividly the first time I realized that my mom was fallible. It was only last year, so I guess I could consider myself lucky for twenty years of blissful ignorance. It was Thanksgiving and we were over at our family friend's house where we go every year. They, like us, are the type of people who favor politics over football Thanksgiving morning, who read The New Yorker, and drink only organic California wine. They're proud Jewish yuppies. My mom and I were chatting near the hor d'ouevres. By this time I was already a bit drunk because college is a bad nagging habit that seems to flare up at any given moment. I don't remember exactly what we were talking about, maybe because it wasn't memorable or because of the Manischewitz. But at some point the conversation turned to my mom's best friend, Heike. Heike and my mom met in the principal's office of my preschool. Heike's daughter, Svenja, had cut off half of my hair during recess. We both thought it was hilarious. They did not. Friendships bloomed between both involved parties.

Between bites of baked brie and mini hotdogs, our conversation turned, as it inevitably did at times, to our ancestors and the Holocaust. My mom is Jewish, if only by traditional, family history, and a passion to honor what that means. She, nor I, were ever bat mitzvah'd and we often skip Synagogue for a family hike followed by brunch. She's more of a spiritual person than a religious one; heavier emphasis on the "yuppie", less so on the "Jewish". But my mom is also a very emotional person, willing at any point to discuss in great lengths either personal embodiment and self actualization, or the pains and scars of humanity. I've been psycho-analyzed more times than most, and even my friends have gotten used to her generous portions of wisdom and insight, mostly uninvited. In my mind these are some of my favorite parts about my mom -- she listens hard and she loves hard.

We started in on a conversation about my grandparents, her grandparents, their struggles, and the horrors of humanity. This conversation took an odd turn when she introduced Heike. She was in the midst of musing about forgiveness and the need to always remember what had transpired in order to never repeat, when she began to tell me about one of her first meals she shared with Heike many years ago. Heike is a first generation American, born of German parents who still live in Frankfurt. She's an absolutely wonderful and caring person who contributed greatly to my childhood memories. Yet, she is German. And this bore a hardship for my mom, a mental block she had to gingerly test before leaping over towards friendship. As they were partway through this meal many years ago, my mom, presumably riddled with anxiety, set down her fork and asked her question. It was a question, that once relayed to me years later, seemed ludicrous, insensitive, crass, and accusatory. She turned to Heike, set her fork down, and said,

"I am having such a wonderful time getting to know you and becoming such close friends. But before we can proceed I need to know, where were your parents during the Nazi era, and what were they doing? I'm Jewish, you see."

Heike assured my mom that her parents had nothing to do with Hitler's rampage, that they, like my grandparents, fled. My mom listened intently and dinner resumed, as did their friendship. She shrugged it off, as if it were inconsequential.

I'll never forget the retelling of that story. I, for the first time in my entire life, was appalled by my mom. I saw that for all of her preaching and proselytizing about forgiveness and acceptance of a single human race, she, like the rest of us, could not entirely forgive and forget. She could not reap what she sowed in the way that I needed her to. Did I really have a bigot for a parent? Or at the very least, a parent with pent up resentment that she exercised on the innocent children of equally innocent people? Did my mom really look at Heike, and see not a caring mother, loyal friend, and most importantly, innocent and conscientious human? Was she really concerned with the crimes committed long ago by a nation of people? What if Heike's parents had been involved in some way, would she have felt obligated to sacrifice one of her strongest friendships to honor the names of our family's dead?

Her words hit me with the force of their implicit meaning. I could not have agreed with her less, something that had never happened before between us especially about something so important. I saw her opinion and her trepidations as weakness and fear. I could not believe that my mom could look at this person and feel instant hatred or hurt because of her nationality – because of something that they could not change. I continued to listen as my mom continued to talk, unaware of the anxiety that her words were causing me. She was fallible. No matter how hard she strove to attain the perfect humanity she had read about in all of her books by the Dalai Lama and Pema Chodron, she was deeply flawed like the rest of us. She probably doesn't exactly remember what she said over baked brie and mini hotdogs, but I will never forget. It was a brief but everlasting reflection on the imprecise and often misguided ways in which we all exhibit and practice our humanity, even when all we care to do is love those around us and ourselves as best we can.

XV.

G. Cohen

It's weird. It's like you work up for this moment throughout the entirety of your life, yet you can't grasp your emotions when it finally happens. You've have had a young, innocent, and naïve life. You hate to admit it, even in the comfort and silence of your own brain, but as the thought jumps around, *bumping first into your temporal lobe then off to the occipital then right on around to the parietal and it fills you up and seems to control your movement, you can't deny it.* You can't deny that up until this point, you have been naive and small, raised in a bed in a room in a house that has fraying wallpaper and faint drawings on the walls of which you penned as a small child and could never fully erase, a tiny Picasso, a van Gogh before the ear was lost. But what happens if when you leave, you are forgotten? And the drawings are erased from the wall; maybe mom and dad have gotten the house renovated and new wallpaper intrudes, filling the rooms in the house that once were full of you?

And, you shudder to think, that up until this point you have been alcohol and drug-free. Okay, you know alcohol *is* a drug thus you are harnessing a redundant notion. But it *feels* different ("okay, mom?"). And yeah, you've had some run-ins with alcohol – truly, you have – but they never felt real against the backdrop of a friend's family's home, taking shots alongside a framed photo where strangers pose on a beach clad in total white. Sometimes you drank enough to feel dizzy, yeah, and you successfully made some so-called drunken mistakes. But you never felt that rush of freedom, that sensation that hits right before the nausea, where you can do anything, you are indomitable, and you are young and wild and free. Never felt that.

Truthfully, you don't know if you ever will feel that. College is maybe too close to home; only a three and a half hour drive on a good day. Good day meaning no traffic. Good day does not, absolutely does not, mean the day you are dropped off. That is a bad day. That was a bad day. It's like all of your fears are manifesting themselves in the form of a doorway, as you are staring at a bed in a room in a hallway in a dormitory that is not yours. You have worked up your entire life for this day, haven't you? Isn't that what your teachers always told you? Elementary school is preparation for middle school, middle school preparation for high school, high school preparation for... well, now you know the rest. High school preparation for college. Or University. Or whatever they call it. Why are there so many names for this place, anyway?

And then the roommate appears, looking sheepish, mirroring your insides. Why can't she at least appear confident? Why can't she be the kind of roommate that knows what she's doing, thus making it easier for you to pretend like you know what you're doing? And shit, should I feel badly for taking the bed closest to the window? She would've done the same thing if she were here first, right? Yeah, she's selfish like that.

Fuck, *stop* it, isn't it weird how snap judgments just happen? Unconsciously, subconsciously, whichever the hell consciousness this is in. But, you think, you are ready to make this girl your friend, maybe best friend, maybe fake best friend. You're prepared for this, you think. You've worked all of your life for this moment, and you'll make this faux-best friend, selfish motherfucker your heart and soul.

But, no. Nothing has prepared you for *this* moment – the one where your dad hugs you goodbye first, and then it's mom with her tears and you make some sarcastic comment about Oh thanks for the tear dye Mom but really you've never felt so terrified as you stand in this hug and it's like this feeling that washes over you and it doesn't feel like the freedom before the alcohol-induced nausea but instead it feels like the nausea. The part where you're hunched over the toilet mourning the loss of your dinner, mourning the feeling you had that existed before the nausea and which seems like you'll never feel that way again. You've worked up to this moment throughout the entirety of your life yet you can't grasp these emotions, no, you can't grasp them at all.

And then they leave. And suddenly a three and a half hour drive seems and feels like a lifetime, as you sit on a bed next to a window in a room in a dorm as they walk down the stairs and into a car that is no longer yours or even associated with you. You actually watch them as they walk away, the hunch of mom's shoulders, the curve of dad's arm as it encircles mom's small frame, fully aware that this is not a good idea, that this is not a sappy love film, that you are old enough to be alone and drunk in a strange and foreign place. And on that first day of college, you are prepared to be lonely. Yes, most of all lonely.

XVI.

Arnold

So it was like 2 or 3 weeks into college, I really blew it during orientation. A girl came up to me and just grabbed my dick. I was in no state to refuse this provocative action, so I took this girl back to my dorm. We started hooking up, and eventually she started sucking my dick. Problem is, she used a lot of teeth and it hurt more than it felt good. As a consequence, I was a little less hard than usual. She proceeded to ask me if I was gay because I didn't stay hard. I later learned that she had posed this question to multiple partners while performing oral sex. As we started having sex, I felt that I was more drunk than necessary. When she got on top, I was pretty sure that I was going to throw up. I thought I could hold it in, however, and it would have been embarrassing to stop the activities and go to the bathroom. So, I continued, hoping against hope that I would not throw up. In the end, I couldn't hold it in, and I threw her off of me and threw up all over her clothes. I went to the bathroom and proceeded to throw up for the next 30 minutes, and when I came back to my room, she was naked on the bed, so I passed out on the floor. Eventually she put her throw up filled clothes on, climbed over me, and left the room. She actually did not go to my school, so I have no idea how she found her friend and made it back. So, to recap, I threw up on the first girl I had sex with in college.

XVII.

Rita

I guess you could call me a…late bloomer. Throughout my earlier years of high school, my close friends assured me that my procrastination, if one could call it that, of this momentous event was 'fine': "there's time," they promised, and "when you're ready," they reassured me.

My more judgmental, and - let's face it - realistic, friends made fun of me, and urged me to "just do it already!" and that I'd be "so much happier when it was over."

Ha! I remember thinking. Like it was so easy. They made it sound like it meant nothing, but every time I got close to finally "just doing it," I couldn't help but remember all of the prior failed attempts of my friends. I couldn't help but hear, and actually see, my mother's words, splayed across my mind like the opening scenes of Star Wars, about how important it was to wait, how scary it is, how dangerous the consequences could be. "I sleep a lot better at night," she would tell me, "knowing that you're not out there like your friends."

Needless to say, I was sufficiently warned. And freaked out.

Once I turned 18, I no longer had anyone on my side. I had become a drag to my friends, who couldn't understand why I was the only one not doing it when we went out on the weekends. And, arguably worst of all, I became a burden to myself: I felt immature, irresponsible, and lame.

At 19, keeping it a secret from all of my friends, I decided to "take the plunge." I showered, dressed in nice clothes, and arrived at my destination right on time. I was nervous – sweating, queasy, the works. I told myself that I could do it, that I deserved it.

To make a long story short, after a few wrong movements and awkward conversations, the day proved to be unsuccessful. I had failed.

It wasn't until I was 20 that I worked up the courage to try again, and finally succeeded. And, although there were indeed times that I wish I had "just done it already," I'm happy that I waited. While it may not be the coolest fact about me, I can proudly declare that I got my driver's license at 20 years old.

XVIII.

Sam

The first flight of my life took me from Hartford to Detroit. I was 20. I was about to start the orientation week of my study abroad program in the beginning of my junior year.

Rewind to two years earlier during Freshman Orientation at Wesleyan, right after I watched the movie *Airplane!* in Butt C with my new friends. The conversation turned to our weird experiences on planes, and mine was by far the weirdest: I had never been on one. As in the movie:

> Ted Striker: *Surely you can't be serious!*
> Rumack: *I am serious... and don't call me Shirley.*

It wasn't something I thought about much. It was just on my list of experiences I hadn't yet had. It's not that I was afraid of flying or reluctant to travel—I just hadn't yet. My family's annual vacations were all within driving distance (even if we drove 15 hours).

For the rest of freshman year, SHE HAS NEVER BEEN ON AN AIRPLANE became a running joke. Maybe the fact of the joke made me stand out from others, or maybe it meant that I had successfully made real college friends who made jokes about me. For a long time, I went with it. At the start of sophomore year though, I'd had enough of the joke and of my lack of travel experience. Never having been on an airplane means more than just never having flown—it means never having gone anywhere new, being tied down to a place, missing out on the knowledge, adventure, and cultural capital associated with travel. Being in a setting with peers who seemed so worldly and did things like read *The Economist* (which I'd never heard of until I arrived at Wes) made me feel enormous pressure and self-doubt. I was frustrated with my inexperience, and the joke only served to embarrass me. I felt as though there was a ceiling hanging above my head limiting my worldview and my imagination. I wanted to shatter that ceiling as soon as possible.

Having the opportunity to study abroad gave me that chance. Study abroad was easy and convenient: the programs provided housing and logistics, and my financial aid made it relatively affordable. So there was no way I was *not* going on this particular study abroad program that would take me to three countries, letting me circumnavigate the world in four months.

The people on my program never learned I'd never flown before, but they did find out that I'd never used a passport. In Detroit, we played a stupid ice breaker game in which a statement was read aloud and whoever identified with the statement stepped into the circle. The statement was "I have never used a passport before." I was the only one to step into the circle. My classmates told me I was brave for embarking on a journey spanning three continents. I shrugged and rolled my eyes. Brave? Yeah right. I was acting out of part curiosity but mostly insecurity.

After all, it was never about the airplane, or that I had never flown before. I was never scared of flying at all, nor was I ever eager to get in the air. It was not even about never having been out of the country ("Not even *Canada*?" people asked me) or even across the coast. It was about realizing that I only knew what was nearby, feeling stuck and claustrophobic. I wanted some stories to tell. I wanted to downplay my naivety and acquire some global perspective.

The funny thing about travel is that it shrinks the world, making faraway places seem closer and more accessible than they are. Simultaneously, our views broaden so much that we understand the world is a giant place and we will never see it all. It's a push pull process of learning about places and learning about all we don't know. I'll always be naïve, but now I'm somewhat oriented. And at least I've been on a plane.

XIX.

Kelly

Bonnie said, "Those jeans look better on me, Fugly." She exhaled a toxic cloud from her Marlboro Light in your face. You noticed her polish was the same strawberry red that you wore as she raked her nails down your left cheek. By the time you made it home your new acid washed jeans were torn on the knees with streaks of spring green grass stains all over, your hair teased and wild from Bonnie's relentless ripping at your ponytail. The contents of the junk drawer clattered onto the kitchen counter when your mother dumped and sifted through them in search of the hammer. She wrapped it in yesterday's *Globe* and used it to smash the glass of Bonnie's front door as she called, "You think you're so tough? Come fight her now!" while you watched from the driveway.

XX.

Manny

December 18, 1997: The day I met Alex and Sandy, 3-month-old Siamese kittens. They rushed to the door of my brother-in-law's house and I was besotted!

Growing up in a city, the only pets I ever had were those that could be contained: hamsters, goldfish, turtles. My mother, who had spent much of her childhood in the country, felt it was cruel to keep animals in small spaces, and would often remark on how the biggest dogs in our building always seemed to live in the smallest apartments. I did briefly have a chick as a pet, rescued from a school biology experiment, but life in the bathtub was pretty tough and so Mickey the Chickie left quickly for summer camp (especially after he pecked my little sister in the eye).

Once away at college, I moved off-campus into a house with roommates who had cats and dogs, one of whom stands out in my memory. Thor was an albino German Shepherd whose ears flopped over, except when he went on alert, when one ear would stick up. Because dogs were allowed everywhere at the school I attended, Thor would happily accompany any of us up to campus and snore noisily through class. Thor's owner needed a temporary home for him my last semester before graduating and so he lived with me. My father had just died, and I found the wonderful comforting power of a pet's unconditional love especially soothing during that time.

Thus, as I moved on in life, I thought of myself as a dog person. Not long after finishing college, I met my husband-to-be, an animal lover who had grown up in the country and was used to having cats, dogs and other animals around. But our busy work and personal lives always prevented us from acquiring a pet, although he would bemoan what we were missing. And then there was the stand-off: he wanted a cat (preferably Siamese) and I thought I wanted a dog.

Cut to December 18, 1997: I remember the date because it was the day before my mother-in-law died. Alex and Sandy had been her 80th birthday present several months earlier, a most wonderful distraction when she was diagnosed with cancer shortly after. I had arrived that evening to be with her and the rest of the family, and when we returned from the hospital, Alex and Sandy were waiting at the door. I had never seen such adorable kittens, and their antics—wrestling with each other, climbing the burlap-covered walls—were both hysterical and comforting in sad times. From that day on, I realized that I was a cat person, and I thoroughly enjoyed having Alex and Sandy come to live with us, as my mother-in-law had wished. Cats have been part of my life since then, and when asked the famous personality question "are you a cat person or a dog person", I don't hesitate to give the "cat" answer anymore. Still, remembering Thor, I realize that whatever the animal, the comfort and fun in the relationship is what it's all about.

XXI.

Jessica

You'd think since I grew up in NYC, with all its great and rich ethnic and cultural diversity, that I would have tasted Mexican food. But somehow at age 24, I had not. In spite of the fact that my mother, who was a superb cook, prepared dinner from scratch every single night (served promptly at 6:30 pm) using all different types of fish, vegetables, legumes, meats and herbs.

In 1975, having completed college on the installment plan, taking 6 years to do so, I decided to apply to Harvard Business School. Since I graduated Summa Cum Laude, Phi Beta Kappa, finishing fourth in a class of 1154, I thought I might have a shot. The day before the acceptance/rejection notifications were to be received, I realized I had taken the wrong set of standardized tests for the program to which I had applied. I felt sick to my stomach.

Although the rejection notice was by that point expected (in the days when such transactions were conducted on paper and by snail mail), it was still received with horror.
I called my two closest friends who suggested we go out for a consolation dinner. They chose a local Mexican restaurant.

It was little more than a bar, dark and crowded, but instead of smelling like alcohol, it smelled wonderfully appealing, although unfamiliar. My experienced-in-eating-Mexican-food friends ordered for me: guacamole, some sort of chicken and bean burrito with cheese and a red sauce, and sopapillas, Mexican fried dough. The food was rich, full-bodied, and savory. My mouth waters now as I think of it.

Relief replaced my disappointment about my rejection as I recognized that I never really wanted to get an MBA or attend Harvard, but I had always wanted to try Mexican food.

XXII.

Roger

LSD…man what a crazy drug: it's been exhilarating, it's been nightmarish, I've had some of the greatest times in my life while tripping, and some of the worst, some moments of the utmost clarity, others of unparalleled confusion and distress; whatever the fuck it's been, I think the Grateful Dead capture it in the chorus of Truckin', "sometimes the light's all shining on me, other times I can barely see, lately it occurs to me, what a long, strange trip, it's been".

LSD is such a mixed bag—spontaneous yet familiar, communal yet highly individualized, provoking deep thoughts and passion to reach higher levels of consciousness at times yet at other moments knocking you on your ass, rendering you completely incoherent, zonked out. Well enough for rambling off these juxtapositions. The point here is not to offer some comprehensive outlook on LSD or provide a cautionary tale, lament on excesses, point out contradictions. I can't say the drug is "good" nor can I say it is "bad". I simply am writing to share a tale of my first time tripping, and to try to give a glimpse of the magic I felt.

I had been intrigued by psychedelics for years before I decided to trip but had never imbibed due to my anxious nature, hearing horror stories of people who'd "lost" their minds tripping, fearing a similar traumatic experience for myself. But the summer after my sophomore year in college, I said fuck it. I was at the Mountain Jam music festival with my brother (our 3rd year attending). The weekend up to Sunday had been disappointing. The music was mediocre, my brother and I were squabbling over losing a backpack with expensive valuables such as his camera and ipod. We didn't have friends who came to the festival as we did in years past. But Sunday was going to be different. Going to a festival is a commitment. It can be physically wearing, it is expensive, it entails sacrificing other plans and obligations. I didn't want to settle for mediocrity…so settle for drugs (man that sounds dark) but justifying acid as a mind-expanding drug made it easier to imbibe. Luckily for me, people in the tent next to my brother and me had a couple tabs of acid to sell, which they told us was "fire" (aka good). I had heard countless stories of people buying bunk acid at festivals, and I barely met the tent neighbor before the transaction so there was no way to trust his acid was legit, but holy shit it was.

The clouds looked ominous when my brother and I sat far from the stage on the mountain and took our doses. It took about an hour to really kick in. The trip was subtle at first and actually never became overbearing. I wasn't really hallucinating but when looking at the clouds I would make out mystical images that I would consistently reinterpret to find new images. The gusts of wind seemed to sing. So many thoughts entered and left my head and resurfaced again. Every moment had potential. It was cryptic and spacey, but also very down-home. My brother and I giggled a lot. Everything was just hilarious—all these grimy looking hippies, saying funny things as we passed. It's weird but when you're tripping, there's some kind of bond you feel with everyone else who is tripping, even if you don't know the people. There's like a secret code, a hidden language. Everything's a tangent yet the pieces flow together in some bizarre way.

My brother and I just found it so funny how long it seemed to take us to make decisions and for things to happen. Levon Helm's performance to close off the festival was what we were looking forward to the whole weekend since it was his 70th birthday and there were many special guests sitting in. The concert was going to be the most epic Band performance since the Last Waltz. And it certainly was. We seemed to wait forever before Levon took the stage due to a heavy wind delay but it was a pleasant wait. We met this guy in his 50s named Mike who was missing most of his teeth, a real hardcore Deadhead who had been to hundreds of shows, who had taken every drug known to man, a real "spunion" if you will, but a super kind guy. He was a perfect guy to initiate us into our acid trip—weird but spectacular.

The music was a bit of a blur, but at the moment I remember it being incredible. I love the music of the Band. It's not particularly spacey like the Dead, so it might seem to have been a weird choice choosing it as the first show to trip during, but it was the right choice. There was so much love on stage between the musicians. They fed off each others' ideas and although the songs were largely structured, within the larger framework, the musicians played in the moment and created something extraordinary. The fans were ecstatic and smiling and moved together in waves intimately connected to the nuances of the music. The moments of joy, for the love I felt for my brother, for the atmosphere, for the music were intense and they were beautiful.

Now that Levon's been dead for a year, I just want to say thank you to him for the great music he created, for his love, perseverance, and radiance. Seeing him on his 70th birthday, tripping LSD for the first time was one of the most special moments I've had in my life and I'll treasure it forever.

XXIII.

Billy

When I was a little kid, I witnessed a woman collapse in front of me, and I had no idea what to do. I never wanted to feel helpless again, so with the help of my parents, I took a CPR class when I was ten. That sparked an obsession with emergency medicine, and in the following years I became a lifeguard and an EMT.

I was under eighteen, and therefore too young to work as an EMT or in any other position providing direct patient care. I was working as a lifeguard, but unfortunately had not had the Baywatch style experiences that I had hoped for. I was determined to use my new skills, and pursued every opportunity that I could find to practice them.

I had started working as a volunteer greeter in the emergency department of a local hospital. A slight step up from a Wal-Mart greeter, the ER greeter signs patients into the waiting room, identifies those who are in need of immediate care, and deals with people who are very angry that they have been waiting for too long. I performed this job with an unusual amount of zeal, and was hired as an equipment technician.

In my new role of equipment tech, I was responsible for stocking the ER's supplies, and that was it. After getting acclimated with my position, I realized that there were many opportunities to watch procedures and learn from other things going on in the ER, there was just one problem – I couldn't do that because I had to stock things.

My new modus operandi emerged. I would come into work like an overly caffeinated hyena, stock the entire department as fast as I possibly could (I actually ran….) and then have the rest of my shift free to learn from the incredibly talented medical professionals that worked around me.

My coworkers were great; they appreciated my interest, and the fact that I would enthusiastically help them with literally whatever they asked. I didn't get to do anything especially cool at first – maybe help hold a kid while they were getting stitches or hand the nurse things as they started an IV. That all changed one Friday night.

I had finished my stocking duties and had done my best to glean any experience that I could, but the ER was slow that night. I was getting my things together to head home, a little disappointed. Usually the department was busier on Friday nights. The squeal of an alarm pierced the air and I looked toward its source. It was the notification system that the ambulance crews used to notify the ER that they were coming in with a sick patient. "Paramedics en route with an 90 year old female, cardiac arrest. CPR in progress" the voice over the speaker said. "You want to help Billy?" one of the nurses asked. I assumed that given the patient's age, they thought this would be a good learning experience since the outcome was relatively fixed.

Since my CPR class at the age of ten, I was dying to have the opportunity to try it. Unfortunately, for me at least, my knowledge of the skill had somehow prevented me from ever being in a situation where I had to use it. I quickly reviewed the proper technique in my head, and headed into the resuscitation room. I would be responsible only for doing the chest compressions in this situation, as the respiratory therapist would have responsibility for the patient's ventilation. I took my place at the side of the bed.

The stretcher rolled into the room. One of the EMTs was standing on the side of the stretcher (on the bar near the ground that connects the two wheels). He was holding onto the side rail with one hand, and using his other to do chest compressions as the stretcher was moving. We quickly lined the two beds up, and lifted the patient from the ambulance stretcher to the ER one. I immediately felt for the proper hand position, positioned my body as I had been taught, and pushed downward. I was no longer a CPR virgin!

I continued to perform compressions as the ER team worked on the patient around me. One of the nurses, who had the reputation for being especially miserable, looked up at me and said, "You're doing it wrong!" "What can I do better?" I asked. "Slow down" she said. I looked at the monitor that the patient was connected to, and could see that I was doing compressions at a rate of 104 per minute. That was a reasonable rate as far as I had been taught, but I obliged and slowed down my cadence. "You're still doing it wrong!" she yelled. I was mortified, I had practiced on pillows and would go over every step of it in my head daily, and so I was devastated that I would be doing such a bad job. I had also worked incredibly hard to gain the trust and respect of the ER staff (most of whom were in the room with us) that I was horrifically embarrassed to be so incompetent.

The miserable nurse then proceeded to come up behind me in a sort of back-hug, put her arms around me and on top of my hands as I was doing the chest compressions, and began moving my hands up and down on the patient's chest. She was not petite, and her pelvis pressed into me as she moved. Would I have two first times in one night I thought? This wasn't how I had envisioned the second one happening.

The patient was pronounced dead a few minutes later, and I was put out of my misery. I quickly left the hospital and ran to my car on the verge of tears. I had waited so long to have the opportunity to practice this lifesaving skill. I had done everything possible to prepare for this situation and I had failed miserably. Not only had I failed, but I had done so in the presence of the people that I cared most about impressing. I was absolutely devastated.

I was upset for almost a week or two after that, and was surprised when my coworkers didn't scowl at me when I came in for my next shift. I took my time stocking the supplies for a week or so – I didn't want to have any free time when the stocking was done when I might embarrass myself again.

The day that I turned eighteen I got promoted to the role of Technical Nursing Assistant. Patient care became my job, and doing chest compressions on every cardiac arrest one of my primary responsibilities. Years later, I became an ER and ICU nurse. I worked as a paramedic. I became a CPR instructor. I taught advanced cardiac life support classes to doctors and nurses. I've done lots and lots of CPR in the years since that day.

I frequently think back to my first time. What was the lesson to be learned? I'm still not exactly sure. Maybe get back on the horse after you fall off? Did I actually fall off or was it just someone being mean to me for no good reason? Maybe it's just that sometimes the first time hurts for one reason or another.

XXIV.

Jon Fletcher

This is the story of the first time I woke up in a psych ward. But it began long before that...

As a child I had very few problems. I graduated 9th in my class, was an all-American and three-time captain of my lacrosse team. Sure, there were some bumps in the road. An alcoholic father, a messy divorce, but I was good. I handled my shit. And if I needed to forget about my problems for a while, well...that's what weekend blackouts were for.

I mean, its not like I grew up in Ethiopia. I had problems as a kid but I was good. I handled my shit.

Freshman year of college went pretty damn well too. I finished the year with a 3.8 and was voted rookie of the year by my peers on one of the best teams in all of D3 Lacrosse. I kept that momentum rolling heading into my sophomore year. I pledged a fraternity, switched majors, even fell in love. To top it off, I was also named a preseason All-American. Things were good. But I never did make it to that season. A little under two months after I was named to the pre-season list, I woke up in an all-white room.

I had a vague recollection of how I'd gotten there: A night of walking through campus, following signs. My friends driving up alongside me, asking me where I was going, me not really knowing. I remember they took me to the hospital. I still thought it was a game, thought at any moment they'd uncork the champagne. Doesn't make much sense does it? Psychotic breaks tend not to.

I remember not trusting anyone who worked at the hospital, except for two nurses with green eyes. I don't know why exactly. I remember struggling against restraints, I remember nurses rushing into the room to help hold me down while they fastened me with more restraints. Crazy people sure are strong.

I don't remember my lacrosse coach coming to see me. But I've been told that he's the one who first told me I was bipolar. The first clear memory I have after that was my mom coming in to see me. Though I didn't remember my coach's visit, it came as no shock when she reiterated my diagnosis. Bipolar, just like my father.

I think I always knew. Somewhere, deep inside myself I always knew. I was too much like him not to be. How many times had I noted the similarities? How many times had I shuddered as my mom berated me? "You're just like your father!!!"

But hey, its all good. I can handle my shit. Wrong.

It's been two years since I got out of that white room, and I can only now admit it. Sometimes it's not all good. Sometimes…I need help.

I spent my childhood believing that my achievements were wrought from naught but my own sweat and tears. In my infantile state, I lacked an appreciation for all the help I'd received along the way. My mother, a single mother of two, rarely ever missed a game. Regardless of whether it was baseball, hockey, wrestling, soccer, lacrosse, football; regardless of whether it was a home game or it was a tournament 6 states away, she was there.

Meanwhile, my older brother never played as many sports as I did. He couldn't. He was busy working three jobs to help pay the bills.

And hey, those were the least of the benefits that enabled me to become the man that I am. Had I been born in Ethiopia, well…no use in speculating.

Waking up in a psych ward is a uniquely humbling experience. Humiliation is a uniquely freeing experience.

We all falter, we all slip, and we all lose it from time to time. Asking for help in these moments often feels like failure, feels like weakness. But in reality it allows us to tap into a strength that no one man can contain. This strength lies in the mystic chords of humanity, the communal ties that connect us all.

This was the story of the last time I'll ever wake up in a psych ward.

XXV.

Annie

My six-year-old memories are more like a flipbook than a narrative I could ever document. I didn't think in words yet; I was just learning to write. But days like that are so far from words anyway, and the more my vocabulary grows the more distant I feel from the things I learned before language got in the way. I was an early talker - I've been trying to catch up to the world since I was born. Sometimes I think that got in my way. I've always *wanted* too much, too hard.

Baby Annie was impatient. I was six when my parents finally gave me my first lesson; I'd already been begging for four of those years. Ever since the pony ride at the fair, since the smile that was too big for my face, since I stuck my fingers in the nostrils and got sneezed on and laughed at.

The hair stung when it got into my eyes; I couldn't stop giggling. She was short and coarse and shedding, a lot. My trained vision now would have recognized her age by the mucous discharge in her eyes, the faded gray sneaking into the shine of her coat, the years of saddles and running and lock-kneed sleeping standing up and sharing weight that had carved out the deep sway of her backbone. Her steps had slowed to sighs. But I didn't notice, then. She was the most beautiful thing I had ever seen.

I was six years old and touching a live creature so much larger than me and I was thrilled like the beginning of falling in love when everything else around you fades out a little in contrast. I was so bouncy in the car ride to the farm my mom almost turned around. I learned how to brush her first. Icelandic horses in the spring are messier than Golden Retrievers. You can spend hours with a shedding comb and have their hair and dirt and sweat in your mouth and your underwear and a brand new colorful carpet on the paddock ground, and it won't show any signs of letting up. I was endlessly amused. I didn't want my mom to wash my hair after because I wanted to be a horse. Unfortunately that included smelling like one too, and although that's admittedly still one of my favorite smells, my mom somehow wasn't psyched about how the aroma mixed with the veggies she was cooking.

I don't remember how I got on for the first time or how quickly I learned to steer or if I minded that I was on a lead rope. I remember that she told me to sit up tall like a princess but I thought I was a king because there was something magic happening that made me feel big and powerful, and it wasn't just the distance from the ground. It's the first recollection I have of a feeling I'd now describe as "becoming." You know those moments - you must - everyone has them - when you recognize the world inside yourself, and your skin has to expand to fit its pulsing, and it's exuberant, and the pulsing is resonant with anything that has ever or will ever be alive, and it's almost uncomfortable because your skin is stretched so tight, but you are relieved, laughing almost, because it's so clear that you'll never be alone.

It seems so hokey and abstract and romanticized when I write it out like this, you know? Because it came before words, and words don't do it justice. It's where words came from, where *we* came from. But it's actually the most obvious thing in the world. It's so basic I have to go backwards to find it. It came a lot more easily when I was six. It comes a lot more easily when I'm with a horse, because as a species, they haven't constructed as much distance between the world and themselves. My mom was tickled by how much I loved riding; the instructor was tickled because I didn't want to get off. *It's okay, we can come back*, they assured me. *Freja will still be here!*

It wasn't Freja, though, although I *was* immediately attached. I didn't want to shrink from myself.

In the years of my adolescence when anxiety made being half a person feel normal and it was easier to have the blinds shut, I tried to get rid of words so I wouldn't be so far away from the horses and the wholeness. When life throws dents in my palms and my skin is too baggy, I think of sweaty horse hair and being a small king and I think of Freja, I think of Freja, I think of Freja.

XXVI.

Jack

There is this one girl named Sarahmantha who got me in a lot of trouble. She had access to pot through her older brother and promised to bring me some over the weekend. Saturday and Sunday had gone by and she couldn't get a ride to my house. She asked if she should bring it to school on Monday and I said alright. She brought it as promised, and I hurried to the bathroom to wrap the package in tissue before stuffing it into my blazer pocket for safekeeping. Later that day, I sat with Paul in the cafeteria and told him what I had. He leaned over to smell my chest pocket and leaned back with a big smile. He asked if I wanted to go behind the gym to smoke before athletics. We got up to leave, and I heard my name called. We kept walking. Outside, Mrs. Bidet caught up to us to ask what I had in my pocket. It's nothing, I said. She said it didn't look like nothing from the way Paul reacted. It's only tissue, I said, and held open the pocket with my thumb so she could peer in. I don't think so, she said, reaching in to take the bundle. She unfolded the tissue and the pot appeared and Paul ran away like hell across the ball field and disappeared. Mrs. Bidet said she was friends with my father and that she was disappointed in me. Then she walked me to the Dean's office. The Dean scolded me further and made me flush the pot down the toilet. He said most schools would have me arrested, but he is a kinder kind of Dean, and so all I had coming was probation. He signed me up for drug testing. If I failed, I would be sent to a wilderness rehabilitation program. I pictured fighting over berries in the woods with crack addicts in withdrawal. It is still an unpleasant thought. School had let out by the time I left the Dean's office, and I went to the gym to wait for my father to pick me up and bring me home. He pulled up and I got in his car and it was quiet at first. Then he told me he knew what had happened. Oh, I said. He asked if I was upset. I told him the truth. I told him I was, because I lost the pot. He told me that he understood, but that my mother was very angry and I should not say that to her. And then we talked about other things. At home, my mother was indeed angry and threw the vacuum at me and said get to cleaning. She confiscated the smoking pipe I had on my desk, no doubt realizing it was not for decoration. And that was about it, on the punishment side. In fact, things only got better for me. My family moved to Amsterdam a few months later. The probation turned from a mechanism of punishment into a fabulous segue. Pretending I didn't smoke became pretending I was old enough to. And that was my first time getting busted. I'd like to take a moment to apologize to Sarahmantha, the girl I blamed at the beginning of this essay. It's not good to blame others for your actions, even if they force you to buy drugs at school and don't warn you about what Mrs. Bidet is sensitive to. Also, I would like to acknowledge the Dean, who found me at a sink one day trying to wash the bloodshot from my eyes, and he looked away. He said I could either piss in a cup or make haste to the pep rally. I went to the pep rally. The only seat left on the bleachers was next to Mrs. Bidet, so that's where I sat, eyes ablaze, and tried to act normal. Also, Paul, if you're reading this: what makes you think running out of eyesight at a small school makes you inconspicuous? I hope you've become smarter about things.

XXVII.

David

Anyone's first time going to jail is an experience impossible to forget. For me, I can vividly bring my mind back to that point of sheer hell almost instantly. The first thing I think of is stepping out of the court house chained by the waist to four guys at least ten times more crazy than the five foot eight Jewish kid I was, there for a few pounds of pot. As I tripped every other step from ankle shackles they make with the chain just short enough to not be able to walk right, it wasn't a good start slowing down the vetted mini stepping criminals. Then I got placed in the back of the patty wagon, the door slams shut, they start rolling and right then I realized what I had done to get there didn't matter anymore. Under our justice system, I was equal to the murders and rapists, and the task at hand was to survive.

The darkness in the back of the patty wagon, leaving just a glimpse of light shining through, leaves you completely vulnerable and it's one of those "oh shit here we go" moments like waiting for the first drop of a roller coaster. By the time they pull in to the jail and unload you, you're not human anymore, you're property. You're property of a system built with revolving doors, made to break you down and destroy you, and it works. If you're not shitting your pants by then something's wrong with you. Luckily, I hadn't eaten for the past twenty-four hours in a holding cell because I stuffed the moldy muffin they tried to give me down the toilet with the toilet paper roll. Nonetheless, I still felt sick as can be and not knowing how long I was going to be in there and what it was going to be like was the worst part. I was being held without bail facing felony charges.

Once I got to jail I recognized one of the guards from my men's league hockey. Oddly enough it was him who had to take me into a room and bend me over to make sure my ass was nice and clean (we both pretended we didn't know each other to make the situation easier). After the naked bending over, they send you on your way with a lovely goody bag; one jump suit, two tee shirts, two pairs of undies, two socks, one sheet, one spork (spoon fork) and a cup. Later on you learn that your cup and spork are your most prized possessions because under no circumstances can you get another.

To my disadvantage the jail they put me in had recently upgraded to a maximum security jail, and now housed murders, rapists, you name it. I had to walk through seven check points before I reached my pod, stopping at each one to wait for the steel door to clink open. By the time I reached my pod and I stepped in there was no doubt that moldy muffin would have left me with only one pair of undies. There was nothing between you and fifty inmates sitting feet from you at lunch tables, every single eyeball interrupting their meal to look up and melt you down with stares. It was like a new kid entering the school cafeteria, or rather, a fish getting thrown in a shark tank.

The guard walked me down to my cell and before he slammed the door he told me this was the cell I'd be staying in twenty-three hours a day for the next week, it's called "the hole, we do this to all first timers," he said. As I turned around to look where I could tie my sheet to, someone called out, "What up brother." It was a white kid I vaguely knew and I guess it was his first time too, and he had gotten there the day before. We talked that night and to my dismay he told me he was getting out tomorrow because his mom knew the District Attorney.

The next day he went to court and didn't come back, but another person did. It was another person I knew, a kid who was always getting in trouble, but was a big guy and I knew he'd be a good friend to have in there. He was a regular at that jail and I guess they put him in the hole because it was his third time back in a year. He couldn't believe I was there and I was lucky enough that he recognized me. I could tell he instantly looked past me being a privileged whitey, but as an equal. He began to tell me his story before I interrupted him, "Wait let me guess," I said and finished his story. The kid they got out the day before had ratted the other kid out for a burglary they did together.

After a few days of word games, stories, push-ups, having a friend with you was nice, but it still doesn't stop it from wearing on you. We talked about all the ways we could retain our sanity if only we had a pencil, but that's the very purpose they don't give you one. The meals they feed you are barely edible and so small your stomach has to adjust. One of the many life saving tips my cellmate gave me was to stash your dinner roll. At 6pm is your third and final meal, and if you don't save your role for midnight you will be up all night with a growling stomach forced to eat anything, which was napkins and ketchup packets some nights.

Shitting and pissing feet from someone's face, in a six by eight cell is another part you won't forget. They make sure to serve you hard boiled eggs in the morning. In addition, they serve no real meat products, but all soy. Naturally the tiny cell turns into a clam baking of the most unthinkable stench. What you had to do was sit on the toilet every time you farted and constantly flush the high pressure toilet to suck the air down the drain. The trick I'd say cut the smell in half. My cellmate said it was the most important thing I needed to do if I were to get a different cellmate. "Anyone else would fight you in here for farting, that's how most of the fights in here start," he said. They don't serve meat because studies have shown feeding caged animals meat increases their aggression, and that is exactly what we were treated as, animals. The juice they served us in a on a cart in a big Jim Jones-sized cooler, tasted like nothing less than a concoction of chemicals, mood stabilizing medication would be my guess.

By the sixth day in the hole there are no guess the name games that can restore your slipping sanity. Every time you wake up and realize where you are, you freak out. You start talking to yourself, singing songs and literally just talking to keep your mind off the situation. Sleep never lasts longer than a few hours because at night, in the dead winter it got so cold you could see your breath and all you have is a sheet, so you wear all the clothes they gave you, even though by the sixth day they start to smell worse than the farts. There were many moments I remember beginning to empathize with the people screaming and losing their minds down the hallway. Once in jail the fact that I had no previous criminal record didn't matter, I was losing my mind just as much as the rapist or murder in the in the cells on either side of mine.

After a week in the hole the guards said my "orientation period" was over and they were putting me into general population. The same fifty convicts ready to rip my face off, I was now going to be rubbing shoulders with, but by that point it didn't matter, I would have literally given my arm to get out of that box. Being able to walk around and go in and out of my cell for most of the day felt like freedom I had never felt before. However, it wasn't long before I could see the institutionalized segregation unfold and reality once again set in. It was just like what you've probably seen in the movies; the Blacks had one corner, the skinheads in another and Latinos, the outcasts. Then on the bottom of the totem pole the child molesters were kept in the same pod but protected in a hallway of bulletproof glass, "the bubble," they called it, or protective custody. "The skinners" or "bubble boys" they called them, wore thick glasses and looked like serial killers straight out of a horror movie. However, it was interesting to see how in jail, the tables were turned. They lived in constant fear for their lives and got spit on from the upper tier every time they went to the library.

My new cellmate was friends with the skinheads, he had some screws loose, but was in there on a domestic charges and I couldn't complain. I knew if it came down to it I could take him. All he talked about was how his girlfriend was openly cheating on him while he was in there and I could relate because I knew my girlfriend was probably doing the same. He got so crazy over it; he drafted a five page letter to her that he asked me to write for him. It was supposed to be from me, his cellmate, stating that he had hung himself in his cell and that he was an awesome guy, that he loved her so much and on and on. It was pretty sick I must admit, but I hesitantly agreed to write it because I didn't want problems. However, there was no way I wanted to be identified as a skinhead so I kept a friendly distance and played basketball with the Blacks and Latinos. After a week or so, either side was hesitant to start a fight with me because they weren't sure if the other group had my back or not.

After a month in jail my five thousand dollar lawyer was able to pull some strings and get me out on house arrest and a sobrietor (machine you blow into to test for alcohol). That next two weeks I could actually eat food again and it didn't take long to gain back the fifteen pounds I had lost in that month I was there. I ate three pints of Ben and Jerry's ice cream a day for three weeks straight; my room was filled with empty pints. Air never smelt so good, but it was bittersweet. Like anyone's first bid in jail, I vowed never again to take my freedom for granted. I was a changed person by the time everything was all over, I had my life taken from me and even though I haven't been to jail since, I still haven't got it back.

Everyday there's first timers just like me, on their way to prison for nonviolent offenses, and their lives are forever changed. In most cases people aren't as lucky I was to escape with my sanity and morality. Sadly enough, the majority leaves worse than before they entered and our communities and paying the price. Until we explore new options on rehabilitation and imprisonment the criminal justice system will continue to grow and thrive, while freedom, liberty and security are tossed in the hole.

XXVIII.

Teresa

The heart has a pretty weak reputation in everyday language. It is easily broken by a summer fling, it flutters upon encountering an old high school crush, it can even be worn on a sleeve! In reality the heart is one of the strongest, most reliable and relentless forms of life. I realized this the first time I held a heart in my hands, and my admiration for the heart has grown ever since.

The first time I held a human heart in my hands was as a first year medical student, on a cold fall afternoon in the anatomy laboratory. This heart had belonged to a 96-year-old female. It was the end of a long week, and I went into lab impatient to finish the assignment as soon as possible.

The anatomy laboratory at my school is in the basement, a large, fluorescent-lit room of 22 tables, one donated body per table surrounded by four students, supervised by professors and surgeons. The room smells strongly of embalming fluid. My classmates and I spent about five hours per week for eight months in the laboratory, dissecting different parts of the body to eventually appreciate the complete human anatomy.

In the weeks leading up to this particular fall day when I held a heart for the first time, my team had already dissected the back, shoulders, arms, forearms, and hands. We'd also removed the breasts and handed one to a neighboring team, who was dissecting a male and therefore had no breast to examine.

My team worked together to remove the skin from the chest and study a few other structures. We then used an electronic saw to cut through the sternum and completely release three sides of the ribcage. We flipped the rib cage towards the feet to expose the mediastinum, a group of structures in the thorax including the heart.

The lab assignment on this particular day was to begin the lung dissection, which takes place before the heart. The heart must be removed first, however, in order to reveal other organs. One of my teammates severed the heart's attachments while I held surrounding tissue aside. It released, I lifted the heart out, and stood back with the heart in my hands. My team continued working.

I stood there for a few minutes, in that bustling bright basement room, surrounded by classmates and faculty, with a heart in my hands that had beat continuously for 96 years. Finally I felt in awe of the human body.

With many other body functions, I have a (perhaps false) sense of my voluntary superiority. For example I can hold my breath until I feel dizzy, and make my muscles larger by working out. I can become inebriated by drinking a Malibu bucket with my best friend, sunburn my skin by laying-out for too long, and memorize the code on a combination lock. Meanwhile, my heart keeps going. I would like to be more like the heart, quietly beating all the time. The heart doesn't seem to mind that no one notices it unless it does something wrong.

During open heart surgery the sternum is broken so that the surgeon can access the heart. After surgery the sternum is repaired but still somewhat weak, so post-op patients may be given a "heart pillow". The patient is told to hug the pillow to their chest when coughing, sneezing, or laughing, as these activities may add stress to the sternum. This pillow is often a large, red, plush heart-shaped pillow. Interestingly, the stereotypical heart-shape resembles the shape of a human prostate more than it does the shape of a real heart, a fact that invariably makes me smile every time I see a cute heart pattern. Give your prostate a break.

Since starting medical school, I have experienced a few moments of panic, at times unable to clear my head or catch my breath. One of the best ways I have found to calm this feeling is to listen to my own heart with my stethoscope, in bed at night before I fall asleep. There's the heart, beating rhythmically, unconditionally, and peacefully.